Passion for Life

Five simple strategies to find the happiness,
satisfaction, and zest you **deserve.**

By Eliz Greene

Embrace Your Heart!
Eliz Greene

"The Red Dress Lady"

The Red Dress Press
Fox Point, Wisconsin

ISBN:
0-9767867-1-0

To my husband,
Clay,
your hand on the small of my back gives me all the strength I need.
You are my best friend and my inspiration.

For Grace and Callie,
who drive me crazy and keep me sane,
all at the same time!

Do you have a "To-Do" list?

Most of us have a list, in one form or another, of things so important we write them down to be sure they get done. Written on the back of an old envelope and stuffed into your purse. Or perhaps yours is held on the refrigerator with a magnet. Or my personal favorite, an array of sticky notes displayed around the computer screen.

- Where are you on that "To-Do" list?
- Does taking the time to care for yourself come last on your list?
- Does it even make the list?

Life is so full of things to do, and short on time to do them, it is easy to concentrate on all of the tasks at hand and miss out on the joy and contentment life holds.

- Are you running so fast that you wonder, "Is this all there is?"
- Are you waiting for the happiness you deserve, sure it is around the next corner or will come after the next project is done?
- Do you feel guilty taking time to recharge?
- Do you have passion in your life? Something that makes you swing your feet out of bed in the morning and greet the day with anticipation?

Or are you too busy managing the details of your life to live it?

Something amazing happened to me when I was thirty-five years old. Life forced me to slow down and I discovered what was truly important. It took something big to make such an impact: a massive heart attack while I was seven-months pregnant with twins.

In the days following my heart attack, emergency cesarean delivery of my daughters, and open-heart surgery, my husband, Clay, and I clung to each other and concentrated on our new family. The girls were premature, but healthy. While recovering from the heart attack and surgeries was challenging, I survived and was willing to endure anything to be able to raise my daughters.

Clay said at the time, "It's the best day and the worst day, all at the same time." We could have focused on what was difficult and disappointing, but we had two tiny miracles to hold. For weeks, Clay and I existed in an alternate reality. In the hospital we cut ourselves off from the outside world and tried to come to grips with everything that had happened to us. While the outside world watched to see if Al Gore or George W. Bush would ultimately be our next president, we hung on to each other with fierce determination and faced our unpredictable future with our new family. Even after we returned home, it was months before I felt a part of the outside world again. While focusing on my family and my recovery, I was so completely content. Who would have figured? Removing the distractions of life, I found what was truly important. I recognized contentment was fragile and it would be hard to hold on to it once I rejoined the world.

Yet, I was determined to hold on to that contentment, not to lose the passion for my family and our new life together. Over the following years, the distractions of life challenged my contentment and focus. On a daily basis, the noise of the day threatens to crowd out my passion. However, I've learned some things along the way, simple strategies for maintaining my passion for life. Life sent a clear message to me: slow down and pay attention to what is good. I hope my experience can help you receive the same message— without the medical bills!

The simple strategies that follow will help you find the contentment you deserve. Today holds everything you need to be happy. Slow down and find your *Passion for Life*!

Walking the Path: My Story

focus on the journey

Where does your path lead?
Has it lead where you expected?

I could not have predicted where my path has led; yet I have found such joy and satisfaction along the way. This was not always the case—I've learned a few things. Mostly, life is not about where your path leads, but enjoying the journey.

We are all set upon a path when we are young, with certain destinations clearly defined. Most of us are expected to grow up, go to school, get a job, find a spouse, settle down, and have a family. For some of us, our careers have a path of their own propelling us forward.

But somewhere along the way, the path gets less clear. What is the next goal? We get lost. Perhaps the path didn't lead where you expected. Perhaps the next logical step isn't something you want. Or, as in my case, the next logical goal remains unfulfilled.

My path began typically, but after graduating high school there were some detours. My attempt at a career as a professional dancer was ended by a knee injury. An interest in meteorology prompted a move away from my family in Minnesota to attend the University of Wisconsin in Madison. There, calculus proved to be my failing. After flirting with psychology and journalism, I settled on communications as a major and focused on marketing and public relations.

During my final year of college, I briefly dated a classmate who introduced me to his roommate, Clay Greene. While the relationship with my classmate ended, Clay and I became fast friends and spent most of our free time together that year. Just after my graduation, we realized we had more than a friendship: we were in love. Happily, our basis in friendship has served us well.

Following my graduation in 1989, I worked a series of administrative jobs before returning to my first passion: dance. As Clay began law school, I kept busy teaching in a local dance studio and choreographing. Clay and I were married in July of 1991, and even though we were busy, we were a happy young couple.

My path then suddenly veered. At the age of 51, my dad was diagnosed with colon cancer. Imagining life without his laughter, spirit, guid-

ance, and wisdom was shattering. Chemotherapy and radiation treatments bought him another year and a half with us, and I was determined to make the most of whatever time we had left. Towards the end, my desire to be with him and to help my mom care for him caused me to leave my job, home, and husband for three months. Clay, being the loving and sensitive person he is, completely understood and supported my decision, even though the separation was difficult for us both.

After my dad passed away, I felt derailed from life. There was no job to occupy my time and mind. I needed to find something new. My path hadn't led where expected and I was lost. Grieving, I had trouble deciding what to do next. What career to pursue. What path to follow. Something seemed to be missing. I was unfulfilled. For Clay and me, the next logical step along the path seemed to be having a child. Well, children didn't seem to be in the cards either.

We spent the next five years undergoing infertility testing and treatments. We visited specialist after specialist, who told us they weren't exactly sure what the problem was, but "let's try this treatment and see if it works." It was a frustrating, confidence-destroying time. Apparently my body was causing the problem and it became harder and harder not to believe there was something inherently wrong with me.

My entire focus in life became having a baby. I put my career ambition on hold. Even though I started a business as a dance teacher and choreographer, I only did so with half a heart because the next cycle of treatments was always looming. Month after month, we charted and prepared, hoped, and prayed − only to be disappointed. It was a vicious sequence of events happening over and over again. So much time was focused on what wasn't working that I lost sight of what was good. We put off vacations because we couldn't plan too far in advance. The fertility drugs made me moody and short-tempered, which was not particularly appealing to my husband. Everything else moved in a kind of limbo until I just couldn't handle it anymore. I'd reached my limit and called it quits.

We decided to take a break from the treatments and live a little bit. We finally took a real vacation. We spent time together that wasn't focused on a baby: volunteering our time, working on an election campaign, and doing things spontaneously (like following the Badgers to the Rose Bowl). It was at the turn of the millennium, New Year's Day of the year 2000, when I realized I actually, genuinely liked the people and the couple we were. I liked the life we had and we didn't need a child to make it complete. What an incredible feeling to be satisfied and happy in what you have. It was a powerful feeling and I wanted to hang on to it.

Shortly thereafter, my path then took another turn. In March, our good friends Brian and Tricia Trexell had their first child. Clay and I went to the hospital hours after Cora was born and as I held their tiny miracle in my arms, I thought, "Well, if this is the result, maybe it's worth one more shot." Toward the end of the previous year, we found, through another friend, a new specialist. At the time, we tried one unsuccessful cycle and I was unwilling to continue even though this doctor wanted to try something new. Now, I was willing to try just one more time. So, try we did with a new attitude, but still I had no real expectation anything would work.

Less than a month later, I was building a retaining wall in our backyard when the phone rang. Earlier I'd gone in for a blood test and it was the nurse calling with the results. She had asked me if I'd had any symptoms or had any feelings about whether or not I was pregnant. I'd told her, "No, I don't think it worked." On the phone, the nurse told me about my hormone levels, quoting numbers that might as well have been in Greek, for as much as I understood them. Clay had heard the phone ring and was standing across the kitchen from me listening to my end of the conversation. As she wound up her discussion of my numbers, she said, "You're pregnant!" My immediate response was, "You're kidding!" She assured me she would not kid about that and began talking about what came next. Evidently, the shock of the news showed on my face, Clay mouthed "What?" I mouthed back, "I'm pregnant!" Clay's jaw dropped and our eyes locked. As my eyes filled with tears, so did his. The one percent of my brain still functioning concluded the phone call, while we both just stared at each other for what seemed an eternity. Clay and I ended up holding each other and crying on the kitchen floor. We truly never believed this would happen, and we knew we had a long road ahead of us, but we were so happy. So happy that even though we had decided to wait for three months to tell people, by the end of the day we'd told eight and couldn't quite control ourselves.

It was that night, as Clay put it, I "spit in the eye of God." I was having trouble believing I was really, finally pregnant and said I wished I felt pregnant. Well, the next day I felt pregnant! The morning sickness started with a vengeance and continued for the next three months. There were days that I couldn't leave the bathroom. My hormone levels were multiplying exponentially and at eight weeks, we had an ultrasound that revealed two egg sacks. At nine weeks we could see two heartbeats. Yes, twins! We had known twins were a possibility, but the reality was a bit challenging to take in. Then we really started to tell people.

Believing I would be one of those incredibly healthy pregnant women who would teach dance class right up to the end and be back in a matter of weeks after having my baby, it was hard to adjust to the reality of carrying twins. By the middle of the second month, I was wearing

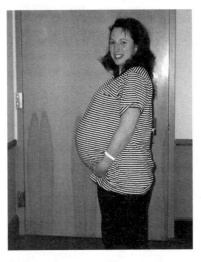

maternity clothes. By the fourth month I had to wear a harness-type contraption to help hold up my enormous belly! Clay came home one day after talking with some of our female friends and said it did not seem like I was having a typical pregnancy. So true. The morning sickness blessedly ended with the first trimester, but just two weeks later I spotted and was put on restricted activity. I had to cut back on work and, basically, just sit. This was not an easy thing for someone used to being very active. In my fifth month, I began having contractions and was put on bed rest. I became an expert at monitoring the contractions. I was allowed to move around for a couple of hours a day as long as I didn't have more than six contractions in an hour. If the contractions started up, I'd lie on my left side on the couch and drink lots of water. That usually slowed them down. The period of time I could be up and around grew shorter and shorter as I grew larger and larger. Soon, I was only able to waddle back and forth to the bathroom.

Then on Friday, October 13, 2000, the alarm woke us at 6:30 a.m. As I snuggled closer to Clay, pressing my enormous belly against his back, we talked about our day. I had a contraction and then another. "Those were kind of close together, weren't they?" Clay asked worriedly. While Clay showered, I timed the contractions. They were six minutes apart and gaining intensity. I was only six months along, but we'd been warned by our perinatalogist (high-risk ObGyn) about pre-term labor and knew what to do. So off we went to the hospital, St. Joseph Regional Medical Center in Milwaukee. We were a bit anxious, but knew we were in good hands. The doctors and nurses were able to slow down my contractions using I.V. fluids and drugs. I tried to be as compliant of a patient as possible. We had waited so long for these babies that I told the staff I was willing to hang upside-down by my toes if it gave us healthy babies. I needed to be on the I.V. fluids while I slept, so I was not able to leave the hospital. I spent the next month in a hospital room, lying on my left side and getting bigger by the day.

This experience alone should have been enough to give me some perspective, but something more lay ahead. On November 12, 2000, I started my day like any other of the previous month: I woke up, had breakfast, and then got up to take a shower. Showering was my favorite part of the day, aside from when Clay would come and visit, of course. Spending the day curled up on my left side, even eating lying down, was difficult; I so looked forward to sitting up and taking a shower. At this point, I had gained more than eighty pounds and couldn't reach my feet, but boy did I love that shower.

Squishing my toes in the washcloth I'd thrown on the floor of the shower, I felt a burning in my chest. Assuming it was heartburn, a constant companion, since I was huge and ate in a reclined position, I was unconcerned. After using the call button on my bed to ask the nurse for an antacid, I went back to combing out my hair. By the time I'd pulled my hair back into a ponytail, the pain intensified and suddenly I began vomiting. Clinging to the sink in the bathroom, I made eye contact with myself in the mirror. "I need help," I whispered, knowing no one could hear me. After managing the short distance back to the edge of my bed I called again for the nurse.

Just then, Nancy Mahn and Pat Brueck, nurses who'd befriended me during my month-long stay, entered my room with smiles and cheerful 'good mornings,' but one look at me caused their faces to drop. Something was evidently very wrong. At first they thought I was in labor, but as they helped me back into bed and began to monitor the babies' heartbeats and contractions, they realized this was something else. Pat went out to see if there was a doctor nearby. It turned out that Dr. Margaret Carr, one of my high-risk ObGyns, was standing at the nurse's station, just steps away from my room. Immediately, Dr. Carr began asking questions, trying to figure out what was going on.

"Why are you throwing up? Is it a stomach thing or a coughing thing?"
I wasn't sure.

"Is the pain in your chest sharp or are you feeling pressure?"
Pressure, so much pressure that I asked Pat to undo my bra in hopes of relieving it.

"Has any one in your family had a heart attack early in life."
What?! I remember thinking, "You are crazy, lady. I am not having a heart attack!"

She began ordering tests. When she ordered a chest x-ray, I knew something was seriously wrong. A respiratory therapist came in to draw blood for some specific cardiac tests and was just getting started when I turned to Nancy, who was seated next to me on the bed monitoring the babies, and said "Nancy, there's something wrong!" With those words I announced my heart attack and my heart stopped. Nancy screamed, "She's coding!" The respiratory therapist began to use a bag and mask to breathe for me. People throughout the hospital came running and I received immediate CPR.

Luckily, Dr. Carr had already paged a cardiologist, Dr. Richard Wakefield, who was on his way to my room when he heard the code called. Dr. Wakefield shared with me how he felt entering the room. "I didn't want to be there," he said. Dr. Carr was standing, scalpel ready to rescue the babies if I couldn't be revived.

The babies, who were being monitored on ultrasound machines, stopped moving and their heart rates slowed. In the midst of all the activity, Dr. Carr and Dr. Wakefield had a discussion about using the defibrillator to shock my heart back into rhythm. Dr. Wakefield was worried it would kill the babies, while Dr. Carr was convinced the babies would survive and the first priority was to try to save my life.

I had no pulse and hadn't breathed on my own for 10 minutes.

Fortunately, Dr. Wakefield was able to shock my heart back into rhythm and I regained consciousness. Within seconds, the babies began to move again. As I came around, I had an overwhelming feeling of calm and knew I was in good hands.

Aside from the heart attack, everything else that day went my way. After I was stabilized, Dr. Wakefield took me for a Heart Catheterization where he threaded a small device though an artery in my groin and into my heart. There he discovered my left anterior descending cardiac artery had dissected; the inside lining of my artery had peeled away from the outside, fallen across the opening, like a trap door, stopping the flow of blood and causing the heart attack. He later described the attack to Clay as "massive," not a comforting word, and explained my only option was bypass surgery.

In the Cardiac Catheterization Lab, I was introduced to Dr. Hussam Balkhy, a cardiothoracic surgeon, who told me I needed open-heart surgery. While alert and calm, I was unable to communicate due to the tube in my throat assisting my breathing. Nodding to indicate I understood what he told me, I rolled my eyes at the absurdity. Dr. Carr came to tell me she would be delivering the babies first, by C-section, and she was confident they would be just fine. I had spent the last months hoping to avoid a C-section; oh, well!

Poor Clay was told far too many disturbing things that day and had already dealt with the prospect of losing all three of us. I asked him once, months later, how it is possible to hear such news and stay standing. "You don't," he replied and described his knees giving out and being held up by Dr. Carr and Pat. As is often the case, it is much harder for the family than it is for the patient. It was the worst day of Clay's life. He was able to see me several times before I was prepped for surgery, and to his great credit, each time Clay came to see me he was calm and supportive. For the first time in our life together, we faced a crisis separately. Hindered by the breathing tube, there was no way for me to reassure him. I couldn't hold his hand through this, I am eternally grateful to the friends who rushed to his side and held it for me.

In a very crowded cardiac operating suite, our beautiful daughters, Grace Catherine and Cathleen Margaret were born at 2:42 and 2:43 p.m., respectively. Dr. Carr describes delivering two healthy girls. "They came out kicking and screaming," and how the cardiac staff, particularly Dr. Balkhy, watched in quiet wonder. The girls quickly tired themselves out and they too needed to have breathing tubes placed in their throats, something very common for babies born prematurely. They were healthy and strong and the tubes were removed just hours later when they recovered from the excitement of their birth.

As Dr. Carr closed on the C-section, Dr. Balkhy began my open-heart surgery. Clay had the next five hours to contemplate the possibility of being a single father of twins. By that time, several friends had arrived to be with him. They supported him as he visited the Neonatal Intensive Care Unit to meet the girls. Clay was never alone and had help as he called family and friends to keep them informed. My mom had been visiting us just days before and was on a plane returning to Minnesota when everything happened. Our friends Juli Aulik and Tracy Goode took on the mission of tracking her down. She arrived home, only to turn around and come back. Clay describes talking with my mom and my sister that day and getting the typical response from the women in our family—be calm, be clear-headed, and fall apart later. My sister, Meg, and her husband, Brad, dropped everything and drove nine hours to Milwaukee, picking up Mom on the way.

Everyone in our lives, including the staff at St. Joe's, was greatly affected by the events of the day. There had been much debate among the doctors about how to proceed, but one thing they agreed on was I would not have survived a traditional bypass. In a traditional bypass, the heart is stopped and the body is chilled. The patient is connected to a heart-lung machine, which keeps the patient alive during the operation. In my case, however, the doctors were certain if they thinned my blood enough to go through the heart-lung machine, I would have lost too much blood from the site of the C-section and died. Fortunately, Dr. Balkhy is one of the pioneers of the Beating Heart Bypass. Using a special device, he stitches on tiny parts of the heart one at a time, while the heart is still beating. It is a new technology, which to date is only used for about twenty-five percent of bypasses done each year, and would not have been available if my heart attack had happened even eighteen months earlier.

My recovery from the Beating Heart Bypass was much quicker than it would have been with a traditional bypass. Once the five-hour surgery was complete and I had made it through recovery, I was transferred to the Intensive Care Unit. Clay came into the room, beaming, holding Polaroid pictures of the babies. I was awake, but still groggy, as I tried to focus on the pictures he held in front of me (my hands were restrained

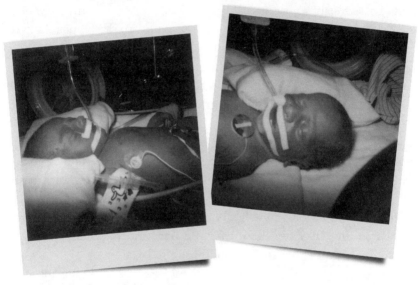

to protect all of the wires and tubes attached to me), one thing came into focus. We had daughters! Early in my pregnancy, we had decided not to find out the sex of the babies and even though someone had told me we had girls while I was in recovery; I wasn't sure if it was true or if I'd dreamed it, because I really wanted girls.

By midnight, just four hours after my surgery ended, the tube was removed from my throat and I was able to kiss and talk to Clay again. Only then did I begin to understand what had happened. I knew something had happened to my heart, but having a heart attack was hard to grasp. "Did they do CPR? Did they shock me?" I asked in wonderment. He did his best to explain what had happened and even tried to explain the Beating Heart Bypass, but it was months before I could wrap my head around the whole situation.

As I lay in the Intensive Care Unit, the nurse kept telling me I needed to sleep, which I found amusing since it was the very last thing I could do. There was so much running around in my head. How did my life become a made-for-TV movie? This sort of stuff doesn't happen to real people does it? As I lay there, considering it all – my new family, the uncertainly of my health, the events of the day, I knew one thing for certain – I had made it through the day for a reason. There was something I was meant to do.

In the time between my heart attack and the surgery, I was aware the situation was serious, but I knew I had to survive. There is nothing I hate more than when Clay is mad at me, and if I left him alone with two babies to raise, boy, would he be mad! He wouldn't want to be mad, but he would be, and I couldn't let that happen. I was meant to raise my daughters together with my husband. That night, I didn't know what the next days and weeks would hold, but I knew I was willing to do anything, endure anything, as long as I got to raise my daughters. I also knew I'd been given something special, a second chance with a new perspective. I didn't quite figure it all out that night, but I knew somehow I needed to give back, to share what I'd been given. I had this vague, dream-like vision about standing in front of a large group of people and talking. It wasn't until months later, when I first started talking about my experience before an audience, that I felt like a piece of the puzzle had clicked into place.

So did I know where my path led? Do I know where it leads now? No, but it doesn't matter. Was this what I am supposed to be doing? Absolutely! I couldn't have predicted my path would lead me to a new career as a heart health advocate and professional speaker, and I can't predict what lies ahead. I realize there are some specific destinations along my path I want to reach.

• Holding my husband's hand as we watch our daughters graduate from high school.

- Crying a little when we drop them off at college.
- Beaming with pride at their next graduation.
- Dancing with Clay at the girls' weddings.
- Spoiling our grandchildren.

Notice, there is a specific order here.

What turns will my path bring? It is unclear, but I will do anything in my power to make sure I am there for the important stuff.

It's not really about where the path leads, it's about walking the path and enjoying the trip along the way.

I've discovered happiness, true contentment, and satisfaction comes not from reaching some large goal, although that's fun too, but from the small, everyday moments that make up life. One moment brought it all home to me. Just seventeen hours after my surgery, I got in a wheel  chair, left the Intensive Care Unit and went to the Neonatal Intensive Care Unit to meet my daughters for the first time. Clay stood behind my wheel chair as I reached in to the isolet crib where Grace lay. As Grace's tiny hand grasped my finger and I marveled in the minuteness of her fingernails, Clay bent down and kissed my temple, then whispered, "Look, it's our family." Yes, what we'd desired for so long was here. Not the way we planned, but here it was, our family. We felt lucky to be together and to face this new phase in our lives as a team.

In those crazy days after the girls were born, I found contentment just holding them in my arms and smelling their "baby smell." The first weeks and months of the girls' lives were so poignant, it was easy to focus on them and how lucky we were to be a family. As I recovered, and they grew, life began to get complicated again, drawing our focus away. I was determined not to lose that newfound perspective, my new passion for life.

That hasn't changed. Focusing on the good things got us through those early days and it still works today. It's the smile across the dinner table from my husband when the girls say something adorable. It's a little hand in mine as we walk across the street. It's dancing in the kitchen, or making my husband really laugh. It's a thousand small moments that would be so easy to miss.

The girls' godmother, Juli Aulik, and her husband, Andrew Welyczko, travel to Colorado each summer to hike and explore the mountains. During those trips, Andrew takes exquisite photos of the wildflowers they find along the path. Some of the photos grace the walls in our home. Looking at them one day, I realized:

Happiness comes in small moments, like wildflowers along the path. If you don't look for them, it is easy to just walk right on by— never noticing their beauty.

So the trick to leading a life of contentment, having a passion for life, is to pay attention to the wildflowers. It isn't always easy, because the path tends to be cluttered with all sorts of distractions: household chores, deadlines, bills, and the troubles of the world. But if you keep an eye out for the wildflowers, you can deal with the rest of it so much better.

Honestly, recovering from a heart attack, C-section, and open-heart surgery had its challenges, but we were blessed with two beautiful

daughters. I knew for sure that "This is IT!" I was never going to experience holding them for the first time again, or seeing them smile for the first time. Squandering this time was not an option. I was not going to miss one moment. Finally, I had my family, not as I had expected, but too bad; I embraced what I had and didn't dwell on what I didn't. We were, and still are, blessed with so many wildflowers. I am passionate about the life I spend with my family and the gifts I've been given.

People tell me I have an unusual outlook on life. I say that's what happens when a ton of bricks drops on your head. Obviously, as one of my friends told me, I needed quite a lot of divine intervention to set me straight. Over the years, I've found ways to maintain my perspective. Five simple strategies to help me keep my Passion for Life:

Notice the Wildflowers
Navigate the Path
Take Charge
Embrace Challenge
Move the Water

In the following chapters, I detail these strategies in hope that you will use them to discover the happiness, satisfaction, and zest in your own life. It is not necessary to master them in any order. You may find one has particular resonance with you and focus on that, or you may use them all. We are all different, but the strategies of Passion for Life will help you tune out the noise of life and focus on what is truly important.

Notice the Wildflowers

happiness comes in small moments,
like wildflowers along the path.
if you don't look for them,
it is easy to just walk right on by—
never noticing their beauty.

Are you too busy dealing with the business of the day to truly live it? Do you feel guilty taking even a few minutes for yourself?

Perhaps it's the dancer in me, but music and song lyrics are a huge part of my life. It's no wonder my daughters and I tend to dance around the kitchen whenever music is playing. There are songs that stick with me, as I am a sucker for a well-crafted lyric. Four lines from a Sheryl Crow song entitled "Diamond Road" seem to run through my head quite often:

Don't miss the diamonds along the way.
Every road has led us here today.
Life is what happens while you're making plans.
All that you need is right here in your hands.

These lines highlight two points essential to having passion for life. First, life happens whether or not you are paying attention. And second, if you don't pay attention, it is easy to miss the good things along the way.

Life happens whether or not you are paying attention!

I used to give a speech entitled, "Life is what happens while you are waiting for things to get back to normal." It is a universal experience. We say to ourselves,

"When this project is done, I'll have more time with my family."

or

"When I get the living room painted and a new couch we'll have our friends over."

or

"Someday, when all this craziness is done, I'll get to do what I really want, and what will make me happy."

The problem is, life is always crazy. But this is IT! There is no second chance to live today. Part of having passion for life is realizing this, right now, IS your life.

Waiting for things to be different or right or normal doesn't work, because you miss today, and today is precious.

The first few days after my heart attack I felt very disconnected from reality. I kept thinking to myself, "This is not how it is supposed to be!" I had all sorts of expectations about what the first few days with my new family would be like:

- Witnessing the miracle of birth
- Marveling over healthy babies
- Holding them right after birth and singing happy birthday.
- Quiet moments with just our new family.
- Making excited phone calls to family and friends.

None of those expectations were met, except one: we had two beautiful, tiny, and healthy girls. Rather than dwelling on what was not normal or expected, we rejoiced in what we had.

Another of my expectations was to breast-feed the girls. During my pregnancy, I'd attended classes and done research on nursing twins. Exclusively breast-feeding twins would be a challenge, but I was determined to try. After open-heart surgery and with the girls born prematurely, was breast-feeding possible? No one was sure, but I was willing to try and would be happy with whatever was possible. At first, the girls were not ready to eat at all and I was recovering from having my sternum cut open, among other things. Not too many patients in the Intensive Care Unit have a lactation specialist visit them, but we made the best of it. It wasn't easy – the girls had to learn to eat and I had to learn how to make it work. But eventually we all got the hang of it. Doing this simple thing for them made me feel like I could do something "normal," and that was a gift.

If you don't pay attention, it is easy to miss the good things along the way!

If true happiness is found in small moments, like wildflowers along the path, one sure way to have passion in your life is to keep your eyes open for the wildflowers and to savor those small moments of happiness when they come along.

While going through a major crisis in her life, a dear friend of mine had lost sight of the good stuff. It is easy to do when everything seems to be wrong. I hearken back to two ideas my father used in his practice as a psychologist. The first is the concept of "awfulizing" – he made up the word, but the meaning is clear. When your path seems filled with roadblocks and thorns, or when the rug is pulled out from underneath you, it is easy to get into a cycle of thinking everything is bad:

- The entire world sucks
- It's not getting better.
- It likely will never get better
- You can't see the way out
- And, well, it's just awful.

His point was that there is always some good, but sometimes you just have to look for it. "Quit your awfulizing!," he would say.

My father was a vibrant and garrulous man. Others sought him out for advice and he was always ready with a good story. He loved to do woodworking and spent countless hours in his garage workshop. If he left the garage door open, it was just a matter of time before a neighbor stopped by for a chat. But, there were times when he kept the garage door closed. I used to wonder why he spent so much time alone out in his workshop. When he got cancer we started a project together: building a cradle. We weren't able to finish it before he died, but I promised him I would finish it.

As I sanded without him, I discovered the joy of simple work. It can be so soothing to smooth a piece of wood, and see the results of your efforts. It was comforting and caused me to pause and savor the moment. It was a wildflower! I get the same feeling from ironing a shirt, smoothing out the wrinkles, and the sound of the steam. There is something so gratifying about it. Sometimes the wildflowers take the shape of a common task done well. Other times, it is the smile of a friend's face when you greet her or the pride in someone asking for your opinion, or closing the book on a project well done. Wildflowers come in surprising shapes and in unexpected situations. Some days you have to look a little harder to find them. Even on the worst days, they are there.

The other thing my father used to say was, "Who's to say what's good or bad?" Without a doubt, I could have lived a good life without having a heart attack, but I have gained a brand-new perspective on life for which I am so grateful. Some people would look at what happened to me and dwell on what was lost; I look at it and rejoice in what was gained. Even the most painful episodes lead us to today.

**Today holds all the promises and all the happiness you desire;
You just have to look for it.**

So why is it that some people face a difficult time in their lives (illness, the untimely death of a loved one, or losing a job for example) and are able to rally themselves and go forward, while others get stuck and never seem to move on? I think it has something to do with being able to see the good things even on the bad days and having faith the difficult times will pass and better times are ahead.

The days after the surgery were difficult, particularly at night. Two days after surgery, I was transferred to a regular hospital room. My heart was constantly monitored by electronic device transmitting information about my heart to a screen in my room and one at the nurse's station. At first it was a comfort, to be able to look up and see everything was fine. Soon, however, it became too much of a reminder: my heart had stopped, and it could stop again.

Everyone needs a sense of denial in life. It is the thing that allows us to walk out of the house every morning, even though we know something bad could happen. Something bad had happened, and I was acutely aware of it. Nighttime and the hospital bed were not my friends. Between the pregnancy pushing out my ribs, CPR and surgery, I couldn't find a position where some part of my ribcage didn't hurt. But even worse, I was afraid to close my eyes, fearing if I fell asleep, my heart would forget to beat. Maybe I wouldn't wake up. Clay had the same fear for me. He slept in my hospital room on a cot because he didn't want to kiss me good night and have it be for the last time. It helped to have him there, but it wasn't until we were home and I could sleep in his arms that I felt more comfortable. Yet, every morning I did wake up, and there he was, my exceptional husband. The mornings were wonderful, I would sit on the edge of his cot and we would have some quiet time together. We would call down to check on the girls and always received good news. One morning, Dr. Carr came in for her rounds to find us there chatting. We felt as if we'd been caught doing something naughty, but she told us to stay put. "This just makes me so happy to see," she said.

Yes, things were difficult, but they were also wonderful. My room was filled with ways to remind myself of the good things: pictures of the girls, flowers and cards from people who love us, and people who came to visit. Yet, at night, I needed a little more. Music helped. The first few lines from Jimmy Buffett's song "Love and Luck" were most encouraging.

Better days are in the cards I feel
Feel it in the changin' wind
I feel it when I glide

So talk to me. I'll listen to your story
I've been around enough to know
That there's more than meets the eye

Everybody needs a little good luck charm
A little gris gris keeps you safe from harm
Rub yours on me, and I'll rub mine on you
Luckiest couple on the avenue

I knew it wouldn't always be so difficult. Better days were ahead. Even during the hardest days, Clay and I knew we were lucky. We were together and we had two beautiful healthy girls. Coupled with all the uncertainty and pain, we had two tiny miracles to hold. There were good things, if we focused on those things we would make it through. At the time Clay, would often say it was like the line from the Tale of Two Cities, "It was the best of times. It was the worst of times." For him, the worst day of his life happened simultaneously with one of the best. Day-by-day, things got easier. Focusing on what was good kept us from dwelling on what wasn't as we'd hoped.

When the path is cluttered, when it is difficult, it is sometimes hard to see the good things. Over time, I developed some ways to help myself notice the wildflowers every day, even on the hard days.

Slow Down

It is hard to notice the small things when you are traveling ninety miles an hour! Days can be so busy there is hardly time to breathe, but I've found taking time to do just that – breathe – makes all the difference. I know it may sound silly, but there is something very powerful about breath. I never really appreciated it until it was difficult to do.

Right after surgery, my whole torso hurt and it was difficult to draw a deep breath. The morning after surgery, all my doctors converged around my bed in the ICU. They were thrilled I was doing so well and I was excited to talk to them. Asking and answering questions, suddenly I felt nauseous and light-headed. Panicing a little, I turned to Dr. Balkhy, who was standing right next to me, and said, "I don't feel so well!" He sort of chuckled and said, "Stop talking and breathe!" There's a lesson. Stop talking, stop thinking, be still, and breathe.

A good time for this is in the shower or just before turning out the light at night. Breathe, quiet the body and the mind, and then, when calm, think about what made you smile that day. Did you do something good for someone else? Did someone do something unexpected for you? Did something make you proud or thankful or motivate you? Where were your wildflowers? Often, for me there is a moment with the girls that tugged at my heart or a kiss on the forehead from Clay. Other days, it is seeing the sun shine through the window as I wake up or the smell of a freshly mowed lawn.

Reflect

Taking just five minutes of the day to reflect on what is good will make a huge difference. This time spent breathing and reflecting is what I call my "Five Minutes for Sanity." As a mother of young children, my "Five Minutes for Sanity" often comes behind a locked bathroom door, yet

How to spend Five Minutes for Sanity

- Have a small piece of really good chocolate (or other decadent treat). Savor it slowly, in small bites. Pay attention to the texture and the way it feels in your mouth. Breathe in the aroma. Be still and reflect.

- Watch the snow fall from the sky while lying on your back in a snow bank. Feel the cold air fill your lungs and watch your breath rise.

- Breathe in for a slow count of ten then out for slow count of ten. Good air in - bad air out! Push out all the bad thoughts and be still.

- Watch a child sleep. Listen to the sweet snore and match your breathing to hers.

- Listen to music. Pay attention to the lyrics and lose your self in the melody.

those five minutes are precious and grant me the continued perspective to cherish my children even when they drive me crazy!

Reflecting on what is good makes it possible to reframe the experience or even change the direction of your day. On those days that are crazy, when you feel pressures from all sides, if you can just stop for a moment, sit quietly, and breathe, you are able to refocus and reflect. Are all the things you are rushing around to accomplish really that important? Can you focus on just one thing and get it done? Sometimes I realize I need to go hug my girls or kiss my husband, because that is what's most important. There are lots of ways to carve out "Five Minutes for Sanity," and everyone is different.

Remember

So what about the really bad days? The days where everything goes wrong and there doesn't seem to be a wildflower in sight? Those days you have to look harder. Sometimes I have to rely on wildflowers I found on other days, which is why I find it so important to document the small moments in some way. Keeping a journal is a good way to not only reflect on what has been good that day, but it also provides a way

Clay's wallpaper

to look back and find the good things on bad days. Photographs are great reminders as well. We have a wall of photos going up the stairs in our home. Each one brings up a memory of a good moment in time. Taking the time to look at them can really help on a bad day. Clay has a hysterically adorable picture of the girls as the wallpaper on his computer at work. I have to think it works for him in the same way, reminding him of why he goes to work and why he works so hard.

Sometimes I just pause and etch a good moment into my mind.

Watching the girls play rough-and-tumble with Clay and joining in to "Dog-pile on Daddy" will forever be with me, as will hundreds of other moments I can recall when I need them. On the days when I'm having more trouble finding the wildflowers, I can look back to other days and be reminded.

I remember a particularly dark time for me, long before the girls were born, when I found it a challenge to find the good things. My plan to be a meteorologist had not worked out. Despite my hard work, I had failed. I couldn't see where to go next and my pride had taken a big hit. I sought help from a counselor and was asked to write down ten things that I was proud of. It was hard; I ended up putting things down like, "I'm an excellent driver." (That was reaching a bit, for sure.) But that exercise stuck with me. Even in the darkest of times there is good; we just have to take the time to notice.

It sounds simple – and it is – but it is not always easy. Carving out five minutes is sometimes difficult, but it is so important to spend even a small amount of time focusing on what is good in your life. I am all about making things simple. To find the wildflowers, to savor the small moments, remember to:

- **Breathe.** Slow down enough to see the good things around you.
- **Reflect.** Focus on what is good.
- **Remember.** Hold on to the memory and use it when the wildflowers are hard to find.

Notice the wildflowers. Don't miss your moments of happiness along the way!

Questions to ponder:
Take a moment to slow down and reflect.

What made you smile today?

Did you do something nice for someone?

Did someone do something unexpected for you?

What did you do well today?

What made you laugh today?

Who touched your heart today?

Who did you hug today?

What ten things are you proud of?

Navigate the Path

*plot your course through life,
rather than letting life's obstacles
choose your path.*

Where are you?
Where are you going?
Are you so busy dodging the obstacles you've
lost track of your path?
Does something interesting on the horizon make you veer off course,
away from your intended destination?

As a boy, my father learned to sail at a camp on Lake of the Woods in Minnesota. My mom embraced his love of the water, and my sister and I grew up near the water and boats. Whether it was sailing small boats on small lakes or chartering larger boats on Lake of the Woods and Lake Superior, it was a pastime we all enjoyed. Clay's family owned

a boat on Lake Michigan and he spent many hours on it as a child. Now it is something he and I enjoy together. We belong to the Milwaukee Community Sailing Center and sail small boats on Lake Michigan. We also have enjoyed several charters on the Great Lakes and in the Caribbean. We can now share sailing with our daughters. They both enjoy the water, especially Callie. "Faster, faster!" she urges. We look forward to teaching them to sail as they grow up.

One of the more challenging parts of sailing is using the chart, or marine map. Out on the water, without road signs and landmarks, it is easy to get turned around and not know exactly where you are. Which is why a compass is so important. Using a compass, or these days, a Global Positioning System (GPS) linked to satellites, makes it possible for you to figure out where you are, be oriented. Using the compass to find points of reference makes it possible to chart a course.

Use Points of Reference

When people say that someone is grounded, it means the person is secure in his or her orientation. A grounded person knows what is important and keeps it in sight as he or she makes decisions and chooses the path to take at the time. Knowing what is important to you and using these points of reference to chose how to go forward makes an incredible difference. Rather than spending your time dodging what life throws into your path and ending up wherever that course leads, you can evaluate your direction and choose where to go. Living life with passion requires taking the time to determine what things in your life are truly important.

People are complex and I think it is particularly useful to have more than one point of reference. For example, well before my heart attack, I had a good idea of what was important to me. In fact, as part of a training program to work in schools, I was asked to write a "Coach's Mission Statement" for my dance team. My mission statement was not about winning competitions, but rather, about making a difference in the lives of those young ladies. Sure I taught them dance steps and coached them to precision, but the most important times to me were our discussions about their lives and the lessons they learned about commitment, teamwork, and time management. I loved working with all of my students, and having a point of reference, "making a difference," helped me make decisions.

However, just one point of reference was not quite enough. During the first few years of our marriage, I was the Artistic Director of a dance studio. It was very fulfilling artistically and I felt I was making a difference with my students. At the same time, though, the working environment was very difficult and the schedule was brutal. Clay was in law school for the first two years of our marriage and his schedule was full.

When he wasn't in class, he was studying. So for that period, it was great for me to have a very time-consuming job. It kept me occupied and I didn't sit around home waiting for him.

Later, when he graduated and began working, his schedule changed. Now he actually had time in the evenings and on weekends, but I was teaching. We moved from Madison, where the studio was, to Milwaukee, for his job and I decided to stay on at the studio because of my commitment to the kids. This meant a ninety-minute commute each way, every day, and we had very little time together. At the same time, the owners of the studio were having serious financial difficulties and at times were unable to make payroll. All of this combined into a very stressful situation. I nevertheless persisted. My commitment to the students and my desire to make a difference for them led me to remain in the job well after I should have. Having just one point of reference, focusing on "making a difference," made it difficult for me to see other possibilities that might have been better for me.

After my father passed away and I started my own dance business, I worked as a choreographer for the musicals at Dominican High School in Milwaukee. Of all the dance-related work I've ever done, these shows were by far the most rewarding. I loved working with Jeff Schaetzke, the director. He chose interesting shows and allowed me a great deal of latitude creatively. It fed my artistic soul and allowed me to make a difference with those students, too.

One very satisfying moment came very early in my work with the school. We were doing a quirky show called *Finnian's Rainbow*. It had an Irish theme at the time when Lord of the Dance, an energetic Irish dance revue, was a huge hit. Jeff asked me to create a surprise dance piece after the end of the actual play. There were more than forty students in the show, and very few of them had any dance experience at all. In fact, several of them, football players and girls who spent more time playing sports than dancing, came to me saying things like "Don't make me dance." or "I can't dance!" But, every single one of those young people danced in what became known as "Act 3" with such precision and joy it brought tears to my eyes at every performance. Each one left the experience with the knowledge that with hard work and determination, great things are possible. I knew I was making a difference! I was also fulfilled creatively and treated well professionally. It was very rewarding, but soon my perspective, and my points of reference, would change.

I wasn't able to do the show the year the girls were born; I was a little preoccupied, needless to say! The next year, however, Jeff asked me to come back and I did. While the experience was again very fulfilling artistically and I felt a real connection to the students, it took a toll on my family. The girls were just over one year old and did not react well to having their schedule disrupted. It was hard to arrange child-care, do all the work to keep our house together, and choreograph the play as well. I was exhausted. The rehearsal schedule straddled the Christmas season and made the holidays even more hectic. All that considered, it was still a good experience and I signed on again for the following year's show.

We undertook one of the first-ever high school productions of *Ragtime*. It was a very challenging show artistically as there was not a great deal of actual choreography, but a huge part of the look of the show was about how the characters moved. The period and attitude of the play required a stillness and subtlety of movement to which teenagers are unaccustomed. In this show, there was no cute choreography to hide behind. The maturity of the stage presence required to pull off the show was incredible and the cast rose to the challenge. Again, it was a professionally fulfilling experience, but the rehearsal schedule ate up our holiday season and pulled me away from Clay and the girls in a way I found very difficult.

In the weeks and months after the show closed, I had time to contemplate my choices. Would I undertake another show? Yes, I still felt I was making a difference. Yes, I was contributing financially to the household and charging my artistic batteries. But at what price? Ultimately, I determined that the cost of doing the show was more than I was willing to spend. Everything in life has a cost, whether it is monetary, time, or energy related. Weighing the cost of doing the show against the benefits, the decision became clear. It was still difficult to tell Jeff that I wouldn't be doing the next show and even harder when he told me the musical he'd chosen, *Footloose*, a show we'd been discussing for years and had just been released for high school production. But my points of reference, my desire to make a difference and weighing the cost to my family, helped me see what was important and I chose my direction.

Weigh the Costs

Since then, using these points of reference to guide me has kept me on course. Yes, I want to make a difference, but only if at the same time I can enrich my family and balance the cost.

Everything has a cost. Weighting these costs, taking the time to examine the impact on your life and to what you hold dear will help you make better decisions. Keeping your life sane is often more important than the opportunity dropped in your lap. Choosing wisely is essential because:

**Saying no to some things
allows you to say an emphatic yes to others.**

At each crossroad, consider whether the choice will support what is important to you. You may be flattered by being asked to serve on a volunteer board, but will it take too much time away from what is central in your life? Will it help serve your mission? Is it worth the cost? Conversely, you may choose to endure something difficult in order to achieve something valuable. Making the decision allows you to tolerate the sacrifice when the going gets rough. It is like riding a bike up hill, if you have a strong desire to reach the top, it is easier to keep your legs moving! Keep your goal in sight, keep moving forward and you will achieve your desire.

Life tends to send things into the path and we must all decide which way to navigate. Sometimes you choose the quickest route to the destination and other times the most enjoyable. Even deciding to ride out the storm, when life throws the unexpected, is a choice and choosing is essential. So the big question is: what is important to you?

- Who and what are your points of reference?
- Is your profession your passion or do you work to make it possible to fulfill your purpose?
- Are you an activist, do you want to influence the world around you?
- Is there a message you wish to share?
- Are there people you want to help or protect or nurture?
- What is the essence of your life?
- Are you weighing the cost of your choices?

Answering these questions can ground you and help you chart your course for satisfaction and joy. Take the time to step back and discover what will help you navigate your path:

- Use **Points of Reference** to chart your course.
- **Weigh the Costs** to decide to say "no" to some things in order to emphatically say "yes" to others.

Having passion for life involves knowing where you are. It's about knowing the situation and then choosing how to go forward, rather than letting life's obstacles choose for you.

Questions to ponder:

What is your mission?

Who is most important to you?

Are you saying "no" often enough?

What one thing can you give up, to spend more time on what is most important to you?

Take Charge

be in charge, not in control!

Do you feel as if you can't control what is happening in your life? Do you feel like you just get settled and something else knocks you for a loop?

For years I've had a recurring dream: while traveling in the backseat of a car, I suddenly realize I am supposed to be driving. Climbing into the front seat, invariably either the brakes don't work or the steering wheel is just a prop and doesn't steer the car. Consulting a dream interpretation book isn't necessary; I know the dream is about control, or the lack of it!

Life throws so many twists, turns, and, at times, large obstacles in the path, it is easy to feel out of control. One of the most valuable things I've learned, and am still learning, control is an illusion. We can't control what life throws at us, and it is scary. I've found there is a huge difference between being in control and being in charge. It is like being a captain at the helm during a storm. You can't control the storm or what it will do, but you can keep a watchful eye for its approach, batten down the hatches, grit your teeth, and steer. I've realized you cannot, truly, control things outside of yourself. But you are in charge of yourself, the extent to which you are prepared, and how you react to a situation. Oftentimes you don't know where the path will lead or why a particular obstacle has been placed before you, but if you take charge and let things evolve, you'll find your way.

Without a doubt, I couldn't control what happened to me that Sunday morning in November of 2000, but I was very much in charge of how I dealt with it. Regaining consciousness after my heart had been shocked back into rhythm, I remember slowly becoming aware of my surroundings. First, I became aware of a tube down my throat. This had been a long-time fear of mine. You hear so much about people struggling to pull out the tubes and fighting against them, I thought it would be horrible. But as my senses started gathering, like an old TV warming up and tuning in, I realized something significant had happened. Obviously I needed help breathing and I needed to let the doctors and nurses help me. I wasn't in control by any measure, but I took charge of myself and remained calm. I knew, somehow, everything was going to work out fine. (I'm pretty sure I was the only one in the hospital who felt that way.) I knew my babies were going to be delivered that day and I needed to stay calm and minimize the drugs they needed to give me to keep me compliant.

In preparation for labor and to keep myself sane during the month on bed rest in the hospital, I'd been listening to music. One CD in particular, Jimmy Buffett's *Tuesdays, Thursdays, and Saturdays*, kept me company. During the four hours between my cardiac arrest and my surgery, I sang those songs in my head and focused on the future with my family. In one of the songs, "Tin Cup Challis," there is a line about going down to die beside the sea. I skipped that verse. I knew that day was not the day I was going to die. The songs helped me stay calm through the trip to the catheterization lab, multiple tests, and being prepped for surgery.

Following surgery, it was hard to find a way to be in charge. Anyone who has spent time in the hospital will relate to living on other people's timetable. The light flipped on at 5 a.m. so blood could be drawn for tests, for example. Everyone in the hospital the day of my heart attack took an interest in us, and, afterward, my room was constantly filled with people who just wanted to talk to me or hold my hand for a moment.

Quiet moments even to begin to deal with what had happened - given all the visits, tests, and trips down to the Neonatal Intensive Care Unit to visit the girls, were hard to come by. Meanwhile, I was also trying to use a breast pump, not an easy thing to do, especially with constant interruptions. Clay says that he knew I was back and was going to be fine the day I posted a sign on my hospital room door requesting that no one enter during the times I was using the pump. I took charge of what I could, and to my amazement, people respected my wishes. One day, Clay stepped out of my room while I was pumping to find my cardiologist waiting patiently in the hall. The sign wasn't really meant for him, but I appreciated his respect!

Sometimes life throws things at you that you can't control. With twins, this happens on a regular basis. You can't control everything, but you are most certainly in charge of how prepared you are and how you choose to react. Taking charge of three aspects of your life: your health, your fear and your needs will bring balance and confidence.

Take Charge of Your Health

My doctors report part of the reason for my quick and complete recovery was my fitness prior to my heart attack. As a dance teacher, exercise was part of my job and, while more meals came through a drive-thru window than I'd like to admit, I did pay attention to my diet. But before all this happened to me, what I knew about heart disease was learned from watching ER on TV. I thought heart disease happened to old white men who didn't take care of themselves.

When first asked to speak for the American Heart Association, I adamantly insisted they not refer to me as someone with heart disease. I was mortified at the possibility that people might think this happened because I didn't take care of myself! I've learned a lot since then.

Then, I had no idea heart disease and stroke take the lives of more women every year than the next seven causes combined, including all types of cancer. I had no idea cardiovascular disease kills more women than men every year. Yet most women believe they are immune at least until after menopause. We women think we can neglect our bodies because we are somehow protected simply because of our gender, and we don't have to worry yet. But heart disease and stroke impact women of all ages. I met a woman who had her first stroke when she was just sixteen. I've met numerous women who have had heart attacks in their 20s and 30s.

Women are not immune!

So part of being in charge is having a body that will get you where you want to go and will be strong enough to survive whatever comes along. Someday, and that day may not be far off, we may know who will get cancer and who is at risk for a heart attack by looking at their DNA, but today we don't. We can't control our genetic makeup and our family history, but there are simple strategies to take charge of how we deal with the rest of our risk factors:

- **Don't smoke:** Smoking remains the number one cause of preventable death. Quitting or never starting, and avoiding second-hand smoke, are probably the most significant things you can do to reduce your risk of cardiovascular disease and most cancers as well.
  - Most communities have help for people who want to quit smoking. Check with your local public health department or hospital for cessation programs.
  - Many communities have smoke-free public areas and are moving toward smoke-free workplaces. Support these efforts and thank business owners who provide smoke-free environments.
  - Today's new smokers are becoming addicted, on average, at the age of just thirteen years! Support the efforts of the Campaign for Tobacco-Free Kids.

- **Fuel the body:** Eating a diet rich in fruits, vegetables, and low in fat, and matching your portions to your activity level is an important part of leading a healthy lifestyle.
  - Most people need a little boost in the morning before lunch or at about 3:00 pm. Rather than visiting the vending machine, plan ahead. A piece of fruit or half of a peanut butter sandwich will fill you up and provide more energy than the sugar and empty calories in junk food.
  - If you must have chocolate, try mixing some chocolate chips with dried fruit and nuts - making a nutritious and delicious snack.
  - Remember the more colors on your plate, the healthier the meal!

- **Move:** Leading an active life keeps the muscle of the heart healthy and keeps the blood flowing. It is not about running a marathon or spending an hour in aerobics class every day. It is about moving around and being active in your daily life.

- Use a pedometer to keep track of your steps throughout the day. Taking 10,000 steps is equivalent to thirty minutes of moderately intense cardiovascular exercise. There are simple ways to get more steps in your day:
  - Skip the "rock-star" parking spot and take the spot farthest away from the door.
  - Take the stairs, rather than the elevator.
  - Take the long way to the coffee room or restroom.
  - Take a lap around the mall or grocery store before you shop.
- Lots of everyday activities can count. Doing less intense activities for longer periods of time or a more intense activity for less time can give the same benefit.
  - Household chores like vacuuming, scrubbing floors, mowing the lawn certainly can count toward your goal.
  - Playing less intense sports like golf, croquet or shuffleboard for an hour is equivalent to 30 minutes of moderately intense activity.
  - More intense sports such as lap swimming, wheelchair basketball, bicycling, running and even climbing stairs require less time (15 minutes) to achieve the same benefit.

- **Make friends with your doctor:**
  - Talk with your doctor about your risk factors.
  - Get help maintaining a healthy body weight.
  - Know your numbers:
    - Blood pressure
    - Cholesterol
    - Blood sugar

- **Manage your stress:** Everyone has stress. Even good things like weddings and graduations can be stressful. How we manage our stress, and how we find balance makes all the difference.
  - Get enough sleep.
  - Set clear boundaries for yourself
  - Treat yourself as well as you do others

Risk factors don't simply add up; they multiply your risk exponentially. Managing even one risk factor can make a huge impact on your health. There has been much debate about whether heart disease or cancer is a bigger threat. The truth is, managing your risk factors decreases your risk for both and other problems such as diabetes, kidney disease and even osteoporosis.

Take Charge of Your Fear

There is such fear about health issues and sometimes it seems easier to put them off – not think about them – rather than face the fear. I am guilty of this myself. As the daughter of someone who died early of colon cancer, I needed to have a baseline colonoscopy in my late thirties. Having had my fill of medical procedures, I was not excited about this one. Would it hurt? Would it be embarrassing? What if the test showed something bad? My fear caused me to make excuses and put it off. Fortunately, my husband will stand for no such nonsense. Relenting to his constant pressure, I scheduled the colonoscopy, and can tell you, the fear of it was worse than the thing itself, as is often the case. Fear holds us all back, but we can be in charge of how we deal with it.

Fear is why people so often wait to get help when they are having a heart attack or stroke. First, they can't believe that this could really be happening to them and then they are afraid for it to be true. If you take nothing else away from my experience, remember this:

> **Stroke and heart attack symptoms vary
> from person to person and from men to women,
> but we all know what is normal for our bodies.
> If you have any unusual pain anywhere
> from your belly button to the top of your head,
> you need to have it checked out,
> immediately.**

The pain in your shoulder or jaw could be the early signs of a heart attack. The blinding headache that is causing your vision to blur may be a stroke.

There is no checklist. You can't check off chest pain, arm numbness, and shortness of breath and say, "Oh, yes, this is a heart attack, I'd better get to the hospital." Conversely, you can't say, "Well, my arm isn't numb; obviously this isn't a heart attack." A whole host of symptoms can arise including: breaking out in a cold sweat, nausea, sleeplessness, balance problems, and confusion. The point is: recognizing something unusual and seeking help right away. Time is critical. Your options are so much greater with the luxury of time. Risk being embarrassed by being wrong and go to the hospital. Don't drive yourself to the doctor's office or lie down and take a nap or wait for your husband to come home. Get help right away. Most people I've talked to absolutely knew there was something very wrong.

Listen to your body and act!

Fear can make us delay doing the things we should for our bodies, but it also delays us in finding contentment and happiness. Worrying about embarrassment or emotional pain can cause us to shy away from new opportunities. People often ask me how I can get up in front of an audience and give a speech. Public speaking is something they can't imagine being brave enough to do. Yet, it is like most everything else. The fear is so much greater than the reality. If you prepare and think things through, you can conquer your fear. Don't let fear hold you back!

Take Charge of Your Needs

Are you waiting for your happiness?
I talk with so many people who are sure it is just around the next corner or wishing it was beyond the current obstacle? But they aren't going after it. They are waiting for something or someone to bring it to them and they aren't in charge.

In some ways, happiness relates to business. If you have a product, you have to decide what price to ask for it. No one is going to give you more than you ask, so you have to ask for a price that makes you happy. No one is going to give you what you need, unless you ask for it, either.

As women, most of us have a problem asking for what we need. We do such a good job of anticipating other people's needs that we can't quite fathom why no one figures out what we need. After more than fourteen years of marriage, I've discovered nothing will drive my husband up a wall faster than the "I don't know. What do you want to do?" conversation. It works so much better when I say, "I'd like to do this or that," and then negotiate if he doesn't want to do it, rather than feeling put off because he somehow didn't figure out what I wanted or making him guess. The point is:

No on will give you what you don't ask for yourself!

Part of what we all have trouble asking for is time to recharge. Often, there are so many demands on our time that taking even half an hour to read a book or enjoy a little peace seems greedy. However, time to recharge, relax, and just to take care of yourself is so vitally important. I often feel guilty about taking a nap in the afternoon when the girls are napping, or reading a book. There is always a list of things to do, but the time I spend recharging myself makes me so much more capable and ready to handle all those things. The things we do for the people we love are important. It is just as important to take care of yourself.

You are important to the people who love you.
You deserve to treat yourself well!

Recharging is important within a relationship as well. Clay and I often remarked during the first six months with the girls it was a good thing we had a big charge on our marital battery before the girls were born, because we sure didn't have time to charge it up afterwards. Whether it is children or work or other issues that pull your focus away from your relationship, it is all part of life. Recharging as a couple can get you over the rough times. Sometimes you have to ride on the charge for a while, but it is important to come back and reconnect. For us, we try to have a date and get out of the house on a regular basis. We try to get away for a weekend by ourselves once or twice a year. But it is even more important to connect on a daily basis. Just a few minutes on the couch, talking, helps. We tend to host family holiday celebrations at our house. I like to cook and it is easier than hauling the girls somewhere else, but it can be hectic. One Easter, I was running at full tilt trying to get everything done when Clay pulled me to the couch and just held me and talked with me for a while. Sure, there was a huge list of things to be done, but none more important. The time together made the rest of the day so much more enjoyable. Taking charge of maintaining my relationship and spending time to recharge it and myself makes me much more able to handle anything.

None of us can control what our path will bring us. Having passion for life means taking charge of what you can and trusting yourself to see it through. Preparing yourself and choosing how you react, but also going out and seeking the things and experiences that will bring you joy and satisfaction, put you in charge.

- **Take charge of your health** and maintain a body to take you where you want to go.
- **Take charge of your fear** and do the things you want and need to do.
- **Take charge of your needs** and ask for what will make you happy.

Be in charge, not in control! Do not hold tightly and yearn for what you want, but rather embrace life, prepare, and get what you truly desire.

Questions to ponder:

What are you doing to take care of yourself?

How do you recharge?

How do you recharge your relationship?

Are you doing the work to keep your body healthy and strong?

What do you need that you haven't asked for?

What are you holding too tightly?

What are you afraid of?

What are you putting off?

What is holding you back?

Embrace Challenge

explore the possible!

**Has life thrown a challenge into your path?
Is there something you wish you had the guts to do?**

Recovering from heart surgery and caring for infant twins was a challenge, no doubt. We were sleep deprived and up to our elbows in diapers. The physical energy it took to care for the girls (with the help of my mom who lived with us for two months), heal from surgery and breastfeed left me exhausted. The fatigue combined with a side effect of

the beta-blocker, a cardiac drug used to regulate heart rate, caused me to fight depression constantly. It was a tough time and it would have been easy to dwell on what was difficult. But each day, there they were, my beautiful girls. Their smiles and gurgles lifted my mood. They were a constant reminder of what was good. Dressing them up, taking pictures, doing regular "mom" stuff kept everything in perspective. We were lucky.

We are eternally grateful for my ability to parent our girls right away - something we know would not have been possible without Beating Heart technology used to save my life. Little did we know my rapid recovery would help us embrace another challenge so quickly thereafter.

Clay is an attorney, and at the time of the girls' birth he was a partner at a private law firm. The firm was undergoing major upheaval: partners were leaving and the future was uncertain. The pressure was enormous and we spent much of our time wondering when the other shoe would drop and which paycheck would be the last. Clay had explored other employment, but nothing had panned out before my pregnancy began getting complicated.

Within days after the girls were born, Clay received a call offering him a job as corporate council for an insurance company. It was a great job with a great company, but we were still reeling, trying to cope with everything that had happened. Clay was initially hesitant; this didn't seem the right time to make yet another change in our lives. His soon-to-be-boss, however, was persuasive. The two had worked together previously and this man was determined to get Clay and our new family into a better place. With reassurances about insurance coverage and a commitment that Clay would not have to travel for several months, we decided to forge ahead. Clay started his new position just six weeks after the girls were born.

Challenge is an essential part of life, without it life is flat and boring.

Challenges come in big and small packages. Sometimes you choose them like choosing to start a family or compete in a triathlon, and sometimes they choose you, like your company merging with another. Embracing your challenge, choosing to open yourself to new things, walking an unfamiliar path—has a thrill and enticement all its own.

Yet, it is how you choose to deal with challenge that makes the difference between wanting to swing your feet out of bed in the morning and face the day with vigor or wanting to pull the covers over your head and stay there all day. Embracing your challenge, facing it with energy and passion gives life zest.

We all have dreams for ourselves. I like what Jimmy Buffett has to say on that subject in his song "Someday I Will":

So whatever thrills you
Anything you love to do,
Just say someday I will

No need to know who
may help you make it come true,
Just say someday I will

You don't have to work it all out
You don't have to tear it all apart
All you need's a place to start

And if it never worked before
Try it just once more
That's what your heart is for.

Whether it's big or small,
If you have a passion at all,
Just say someday I will
Someday

We all dream of something, but how do you turn "someday" into this day? Embracing challenge means choosing to do something you don't really know you can accomplish, doing your homework and jumping into it with passion and determination.

There are risks, no question. The larger the challenge you face, the bigger the risks. No one likes to look foolish and we all do our best to avoid embarrassment. Nevertheless, sometimes it is worth the risk of being embarrassed, being wrong or having things not work out as planned to try something new. Learning to sail is difficult because it can take so long to understand all the concepts happening at the same time: wind, sail, keel, and rudder. Sailing is a constant lesson in humility; the wind tosses around even the best sailors. Doing anything new, especially something physical, involves risk. Challenges involving career or financial issues carry even higher risks. Since the girls were born, I've found some ways to help me embrace my challenges (those of my choosing and those that fell in my path). I hope my sharing them will encourage you to embrace your own.

Embrace a Sense of Humor

A few years back, I was asked to throw out the first pitch at a major league baseball game. Even with all my dance training, I have never been particularly sporty and really had no business being involved with any sport involving throwing or catching a ball. Clay tried, early in our relationship, to teach me to play softball, but after the ball rolled out of my glove, down my arm and smashed my sunglasses, he finally understood the problem. My contribution to the softball league was keeping score — at which I am quite good. Nevertheless, how many people get to throw the first pitch? It sounded like fun.

Clay thought I was nuts. He was sure that I would throw the ball into the dirt and people would boo me. "They booed the president; why wouldn't they boo you?" he exclaimed. I decided I didn't care. It was worth the risk to have such a unique experience.

Clay, good sport that he is, bought me a baseball for Mother's Day and started coaching me. We measured off the distance across the front yards and he (and the neighbors) gave me pitching lessons and encouragement. I practiced and was able to throw a decent ball. Right up to the moment I walked out on the field, Clay was incredibly supportive; he'd embraced my challenge, too. He kept telling me, "Block out everything else. Just focus on the catcher. Keep looking at the catcher and you'll do just fine. You can do this." We talked about where to stand, and I was ready. After shaking hands with the catcher, I prepared to walk out on the field.

As we started out onto the field, the catcher turned to me and said, "Good luck. I'm not wearing a cup. Don't hurt me!" and then ran off for home plate. Chuckling, I walked to the pitcher's mound. As I turned and he nodded that we were ready, I laughed harder. As I tried to focus, he squatted and assumed the catcher position — I couldn't really look at him. His words kept echoing in my head, "I'm not wearing a cup ... I'm not wearing a cup." It was time, and I threw the ball. I'm not sure exactly ly what happened but the ball went kind of sideways and ended up bouncing and rolling to the first base line. On the giant screen, my name and "survived a heart attack while pregnant with twins" flashed up. So

rather than boos, I heard thousands of people go "Aww…" My husband says they all thought I'd sustained some sort of disability from my heart attack. Rather than being embarrassed, I found the whole thing very funny. I know I haven't always had a sense of humor about myself, but I've found it essential when embracing new challenges.

When I got pregnant and knew there was a possibility we'd have twins, some of my friends started teasing me immediately about how big I would get. They made jokes about having to use a boatlift to get me aboard a sailboat or rolling me up the stairs. As I got larger and larger, I became more and more of a klutz. Even my mom began to joke that I should have an alarm like trucks have when they back up. I learned quickly to laugh at myself and it turned out to be an important lesson for the time ahead. Our family has a saying: "If you can laugh about it, it can't be that bad." It's true.

These are light-hearted examples of a bigger point: having a sense of humor, not taking things too seriously when they don't work out exactly as planned is essential.

**We all make mistakes, but the biggest mistake is never trying!
The biggest risk is not taking one!**

Embrace a sense of humor, and risk being wrong or looking foolish. Things may not work out exactly as you planned. What do you wish you could do, but are worried to try? Try, without risk there is no zest!

Embrace the Unknown

Like fear of embarrassment, fear of the unknown can hold you back, but like the dreaded medical exam, things rarely turn out to be even close to as bad as you fear. I admire people who look at a new challenge or opportunity and think about how to make it work, rather than dwell on the reasons why it shouldn't. Oftentimes when we face an uncertain situation, the fear of the unknown holds us back. We all would prefer a guarantee, to know exactly how things will work out, but life is hard to predict. We have to make choices without reassurances, or we miss out. True courage is being afraid of something, but doing it any way.

My mom is one of the most courageous people I know. When I was in high school, she was very unhappy in her career. She decided to leave her job, go back to school, and pursue something new. It was all uncharted territory for her. It also meant a lot of sacrifice. The school was an hour away and she knew no one, but she embraced the challenge and loved it. She became a travel agent, and not long thereafter, bought her own agency. With the support of our family, she continued to embrace new experiences and fulfilled one of her lifelong dreams by traveling to Peru and visiting Machu Picchu. She knew no one on the trip, but embraced the adventure wholeheartedly.

She faced the challenge of being widowed after thirty years of marriage with the same determination and grace. She, in the matter of a few years, lost her husband, retired, sold her business, and moved to a new city. For some, those challenges would have been too much, for her they were part of life. When I asked her if she really wanted to leave her friends and move closer to us she said, "I can make friends anywhere." She can, and did. She is amazing.

Periodically, I speak to doctors and medical students about my experience and the gratitude I feel for Dr. Balkhy's willingness to embrace new technology and his courage to use it on me. I've had a number of conversations with him about the Beating Heart technology. He originally used it only on his sickest patients, those who had multiple organs in jeopardy or failing completely. As his experience with the Beating Heart technology grew and he saw the positive results, he embraced the technology for more and more patients and began to use it on the majority of his bypass patients. However, I didn't really fit the profile of a good candidate for beating heart bypass. Later, other surgeons told me they would have been reluctant to do a Beating Heart Bypass on a patient who's heart had recently stopped. I am eternally grateful that Dr. Balkhy trusted his clinical judgment and surgical skills enough to embrace the technology and save my life. He is my hero, too.

Trust in your abilities and have the courage to face the unknown!

Embrace the Difficult

The summer after the girls' third birthday, my neighbor and good friend Kelly Heil and I were looking forward to months of fun with the kids. She and her husband, Bob, have three children: a teenaged son, a daughter less than a year older than our girls, and a son just ten months younger. Both families had invested in backyard swing sets and we had plans for sunny days, walks, and trips to the pool. Clay and I had done a great deal of work on the house and yard over the preceding year and had even purchased new furniture and had the interior painted. After nearly ten years in the house, we had finally completed all the improvements! We were done. I was so happy. In a matter of weeks, Clay came home and announced it was time for us to move. What?!

I loved our house and our neighbors. We'd discussed moving in the past, since we wanted better schools for the girls and knew it was just a matter of time, but had decided we would wait until the girls were ready for first grade. That was years away. But he was very persuasive and had valid arguments about interest rates and home values. Ultimately, he was right. It was the right time to move, but I was not happy about it. The financial pressure of increasing our mortgage when I wasn't working was worrisome. Lamenting leaving Kelly and moving further away from my mom, I dwelled on all that was difficult. The more I dragged my feet, the worse the anxiety became. My stomach was constantly in knots.

Finally, as we were forced to decide between the possibility of paying two mortgages and a bridge loan or losing the new house we found, it became too much. The pain, which had been in the center of my chest for days, began to radiate up to my jaw. It was frightening, I wasn't sure what was happening and the thought it might be another heart attack made it even worse. Every year, I stand before thousands of people and say, "if you have unusual pain anywhere from your waist on up, you need to get it check out immediately." So even though I was 99% sure the pain was not another heart attack, I went to the emergency room. As it turns out, I was right, it wasn't cardiac related. I had given myself stress-induced reflux, not a heart attack. But it frightened me into a realization. I had allowed my anxiety to affect my health; so how long would it be before it affected my heart? I knew something had to change: I needed to embrace the move.

In the midst of all the difficulties, I could not see the possible. But I realized that needed to change. I stopped dwelling on what I couldn't change and focused on what I could. Rather than worry (despite Clay's careful computations) about how we would afford to triple our mortgage while I wasn't working, I started to think about ways I could bring income into the household and still be the mom I want to be. As it turns out, I developed a brand-new career for myself as a heart health advocate and professional speaker, all because I embraced a move I didn't want to make.

It is so much easier to see the problems in a situation, than to discover the possibilities. Taking a step back, looking at things from a different perspective may give you insight you didn't have before.

Don't dwell on the difficult, explore the possible!

Embrace the Motivation

We all need challenge in our lives; otherwise, life becomes flat and passionless. I am all for having balance and keeping sanity in my life, but sometimes it is hard to do what you need to do without challenge, a sense of risk, and the need to try a bit harder.

After surgery, exercise was essential to my recovery and to protect myself against further problems, but I had difficulty following through. After "graduating" from a cardiac rehabilitation program, I was supposed to go home and exercise on my own. You would think having a heart attack at age thirty-five would be enough motivation to make me want to work out. It wasn't.

The motivation came when Clay sat me down at the kitchen table one evening after we put our then six-month-old twins to bed. He had been through a great deal those past six months (and the months before that, when I was pregnant). No husband should have to face the prospect of losing his wife and unborn twin babies all in one moment. Fortunately, we all survived. Sadly, there is no surgery to repair the scars Clay carries. While I struggled with my recovery, he struggled with the constant worry that it could happen again. Clay told me he was concerned I was not doing the work to fully recover, since it appeared to him I was only making a rather lackluster attempt to exercise.

"I just can't find the time," I told him. There was a litany of things I needed to do every day, things that were important and took up all my time: the laundry, the shopping, the cleaning, the cooking, etc. Those things and caring for the girls left me tired all the time. What I left out was I also hated exercising. Even though I'd always been active, now I just hated it. Before the girls were born, I had been a dance teacher and was quite fit. At that time, I hadn't had to make special time to work out; it was just part of what I did during my day. Now I was tired and dragging around an extra fifty pounds. It was all I could do to carry the girls one at a time into the house and then carry in the groceries. How was I going to get a workout in too? I knew I should be doing it; I just couldn't force myself to get going.

Clay looked me in the eye and said the words that gave me the kick in the pants I needed: "Honey, nothing else you do makes any difference to the girls and me unless you are here. You are our whole world. You need to do the work to be sure you are still around."

There was no comeback and no more excuses. If I didn't take care of myself, how could I take care of the people I loved? If I didn't take care of myself, how would I be part of their future? In quick flashes, I saw all of the things I wanted to share with Clay in the future: Holding his hand as we watch the girls graduate from high school and later college. Dancing with him at their weddings. Watching the sunset from the back of the sailboat we could afford sometime after paying for college and weddings. Playing with our grandchildren. I don't want to miss any of those moments, or any of the other good and bad moments for a long, long time. I'd found my motivation, but I still needed a plan.

For years, Clay has worked out every day. For him, the every-other day or three-times-a-week plan just never worked. It was too easy to put it off until the next day, and the next day. After losing his stepfather and then my father to cancer, he made the commitment to himself to exercise every day. So he challenged me. He told me that if I could exercise for at least twenty minutes every day for one hundred days, he'd buy me anything I wanted. (He knew, of course, that I would never ask for anything too extravagant!)

Not only did I have the motivation, I also had a challenge and I accepted it. It wasn't easy. I realized, however, it was worth investing twenty or thirty minutes of my day to have a body that will take me where I want to go. At that time, we had a bike stand/trainer in the house, so I used that on days when I couldn't go out and walk outside. I also walked in the mall. But I was doing something every day and the days were building up. I made it eighty days and then got the flu and missed a day. But my motivation was still there and so was the challenge. I started again from zero the very next day, and this time I made it. Somewhere along the line, it became more of a decision not to exercise, than to go ahead and work out. Exercising became a matter of when in the day I was going to do it, rather than whether I would. It just became part of my life and I kept going and going. And I felt better and better. I was doing the work.

While I was getting stronger, I was setting an example for my girls on living a healthy life. Have I missed a day since then? Of course I have. But it is not about perfection; it's about a lifetime habit. Being more active every day. I always go back to it. Over the years, many other people have used the simple program detailed in my book *The 100-Day Challenge* to find the motivation and make a change in their own lives. *The 100-Day Challenge* has a simple premise. Make a commitment to your health. Set a specific and reasonable daily goal (for example 20 minutes or 8,000 steps per day) and complete that goal every day for 100 days in a row. It works! Anyone can use it to build a healthy habit for life.

Admittedly, however, *The 100-Day Challenge* hasn't always been enough for me. After accumulating more than eight hundred days, I came down with pneumonia and was in bed for days. It was bad. I broke my streak of daily exercise and had a hard time going back to it. I knew I could do it, so I wasn't as motivated. The challenge was gone.

Around the girls' third birthday, both Kelly and I were finding ourselves less than motivated. We both had friends who had done the Chicagoland Danskin Triathlon and raved about the experience. Kelly and I had been walking together with our kids for more than a year and she was a "100 Day Challenge" convert as well. We both felt we needed a new challenge. We started talking about participating in the next season's event in July of 2004.

Clay didn't like the idea one bit. He was very worried about my keeling over in the process. I was concerned as well, but my cardiologist, after a stress test, gave me his approval and we devised a training plan that would be safe for me. Neither Kelly nor I truly knew if we could finish the triathlon, and that was our goal: just to cross the finish line together. We started training fourteen weeks before the race. We'd been walking together for a long time, and we'd decided that we'd walk the 3.5 mile run, so that didn't concern us. We knew biking 12.5 miles would be difficult, but we were confident we could do that part. The half-mile swim was less of a concern for Kelly, who had been on the high school swim team. I, however, thought there was a real possibility I might drown, especially after our first day in the pool! I swam one length of the pool and thought I was going to puke. I really didn't know if I could do it. When we added together all the elements of the triathlon-the swim, the bike, and the run – it seemed monumental.

With my doctor's blessing, and eventually Clay's, Kelly and I dove into our training. It was difficult in the beginning, but we learned a lot and it got easier. There is a joy in discovering your body's potential for work. There is a beauty in doing something better than you did before. There were hard days and there were days when we were proud. We always ended with a high-five and the knowledge we were in this together, and we had our husbands right behind us.

Very early on the morning of the triathlon, I met Kelly in the middle of our street. It was still dark and it was a little chilly for a July morning. We were so nervous! We each had packed our kids off to their respective grandmas the night before, but neither of us had slept well. Kelly and I climbed into the backseat and Bob and Clay took the front for the hour-long drive to Pleasant Prairie, Wisconsin. The parking lots were full when we arrived at 5:30 a.m.

The Danskin Triathlon is a women-only event and benefits breast cancer research. Women of all walks of life were there to compete. There were elite athletes and women who had never exercised before deciding to train for the event. Some participants were breast cancer survivors, some still undergoing treatment – they were the most inspirational. There was an atmosphere of sisterhood, excitement and anxiety. The "old timers" encouraged the "newcomers." As we left Clay and Bob in the parking lot and boarded the bus to the start, we knew we were prepared. Yet, we were anxious. We focused on our goal: finishing.

Clay and Bob spent the day following us from venue to venue. They found us before the start of the swim with hugs and encouragement. As we stood in the water waiting for our turn to start the swim, Kelly turned to me and said, "See you on the other side!" We'd decided to meet up in the transition area, by our bikes. Kelly is a much faster swimmer than I, and there was no way for us to stay together in the water. So off we went. As I breaststroked across the lake, I kept repeating to myself, "I can do this, I can do this." I knew Kelly was on the other side waiting for me. I knew this would be the biggest challenge of the day, and I knew my body was capable of getting me to the other side. As I exited the water, I heard Clay cheering and calling my name. To my surprise, there was Kelly; she had waited for me at the water's edge, not by our bikes as we had planned. As she had exited the water, she had seen another woman's t-shirt that read, "Start the race together. End the race together." She stopped right there and waited for seven minutes until I emerged from the water. I was delighted to see her. With a high-five to celebrate the end of the swim, we ran to get on our bikes. We were on our way.

Even though we'd declared that our goal was just to finish, something happened to Kelly during the bike portion of the race. We both were riding road bikes, while most of the other women around us were riding

much heavier mountain bikes. As we approached hills, we were able to pass the women on the heavier bikes. It was invigorating. It was evidently intoxicating to Kelly. Suddenly she was riding harder and yelling, "Passing on your left!" at every opportunity. She led the way and I did my best to keep up. As we crested hills, I would look forward to the coast down the other side. But Kelly would start pedaling as soon as she could and we gained more and more speed. I did my best to keep up. On one particular hill, we crested going twenty-five miles an hour – I stopped looking at the speed on the way down – I was more concerned about crashing.

We finished the bike portion and began the run. That transition is difficult, as anyone who has tried to walk after riding a bike would know.

Your legs don't work very well initially. We had finished the first two parts of the race and knew we would finish. Kelly and I spent part of the time talking to a woman who easily weighed more than three hundred pounds. There we were, a mile and a half from the finish line and we all knew we were going to finish. She was so joyful. She had lost 80 pounds since the time she committed to doing the race and was so proud of herself. If she can do it, and I can do it, anyone can.

Kelly and I even managed to run during part of the race and finished the in two hours and two minutes – a time we knew we could beat next time. It was a great experience and I encourage everyone to give it a try.

We were both bitten by the triathlon bug, as was Clay. The following season Clay competed in his first triathlon, finishing second in his age division - show off! Kelly and I decided to compete in our individual age divisions during the 2005 Danskin. I started about fifteen minutes before she did and was motivated to keep going by the fact that she might catch me. She didn't. I finished the race in an hour and forty-four minutes, cutting seventeen minutes off my previous time. Kelly finished in four minutes less. Our friendly competition keeps us motivated to keep training. Triathlons are part of our lives now. My goal is to compete in three or four sprint distance triathlons per season. Clay is working his way up to an Ironman Triathlon, which includes a 2.4-mile swim, 112-mile bike and a 26.2-mile run. He is a little crazy! The girls have become expert spectators and look forward to when they can race like Mommy and Daddy.

Is there something you desire or need? What will motivate you to achieve it? Finding a challenge makes achieving a goal more exciting.

Use challenge to motivate yourself!

Having passion for life means being excited about what you are doing. Embracing new challenges is thrilling and empowering. What are you waiting for? What is holding you back? Today is the day. Don't waste any more time on fear and worry. Do your homework and plunge in. We all face those moments when we stand at the cliff's edge wondering what lies below. I say JUMP! Jump with joy in your heart and passion in your life. Do a triathlon or take your own 100-Day Challenge. Start the book, go back to school, cut your hair, or pitch the ball.

- **Embrace a sense of humor** and don't let the chance things might not work out stop you.
- **Embrace the unknown,** have courage to face the adventure.
- **Embrace the difficult** and focus on the possible.
- **Embrace the motivation** and get what you deserve.

Whether it's big or small, if you have a passion at all, promise yourself and say, "TODAY I will!"

Questions to ponder:

What do you yearn for?

What have you always wanted to try?

What is holding you back?

How can you embrace your challenge?

Move the Water

be a positive force in the world.

Are you fishing for misery or trolling for joy?

Perhaps it's the sailor in me, but I love the image of a sailboat cutting through the tranquil water, leaving behind a wake that rolls away to the shore. I like to think of myself cutting a wake through the world in the same way: moving the water and affecting those around me in a positive way. Those who live passionately leave a wake of positive influence behind them. I've found my attitude toward the world and the people in it makes a huge difference on how I view what happens to me. If you go around thinking it's going to be a bad day, it probably will be. If you go around looking for good things, you'll likely find them. You can either go fishing for misery or troll for joy. What you catch depends on the bait you're using.

Be a Positive Force

Opportunities to move the water in small ways are everywhere. Think about how many times a day someone asks, "How are you?" or "How are things?" Now we all know this isn't an invitation to launch into a full medical history, but the way such questions are answered makes a big difference in how the rest of the conversation will go. Lots of us just answer "Fine." Some of us put a little sigh in there letting the other person know, "I'm saying I'm fine, but I don't really mean it." Others will answer in many ways that put you off like, "I'm swamped, "Tired," or any number of negative responses. I worked with one gentleman who always responded, "Normal." Which, over time, I began to believe was not necessarily true!

I view "How are you?" as an opportunity to be positive. I'll respond, "Peachy," or "Ducky," which are always certain to get a chuckle. My response is a way to pass along some good feelings. Even on days when I'm feeling pressure I'll say something like, "Crazy busy, but I'm happy to hear from you." I like to experiment, especially when visiting somewhere new. While walking down the street or a hallway and simply smile at people. It is interesting to see people's reactions. Some just smile back, others look away and speed up, some may even turn around to see if you are actually smiling at them. It is just another way of being positive in the world. The positive energy you project will come back to you.

But being a positive force is about more than a simple greeting, or a smile, it is about connecting with the people around you in a positive, affirming way. True passion for life is best expressed when it is reflected back to you. Sharing your passion and your life allows so much joy into your life. There are many ways to connect, I've found a few to help keep my Passion for Life:

Have a Grateful Heart

Along with projecting a positive attitude, noticing what is good in your life and being grateful for all those things is a real gift. The girls' godmother, Juli, is the quintessential definition of "well-mannered." She must write the "thank you" note in the car on the way home from an event; the note always arrives perfectly worded and without fail. I try to be good about "thank you" notes, but I also try to be grateful in other ways.

Because, being grateful is more than just acknowledging the things given to you. It's about valuing and appreciating your relationships and the support you receive. People do things, even small things, which have a profound effect. It is important to recognize them and be grateful. We have so many examples in the first day of the girls' lives:

- Our friends who rushed to Clay's side to support him.
- My sister and her husband dropping everything, driving for hours, picking Mom up, and driving even more hours to be with us.
- My brother-in-law, Brad, standing at the end of my bed in the intensive care unit while my sister, mom and Clay were elsewhere, just chatted with me about children. It was so normal and so odd at the same time. No one else was talking to me about normal things at that point. What a gift.
- The Intensive Care Nurse who made it her personal mission on the day after my surgery to get me out of bed and to the Neonatal Intensive Care Unit to meet my daughters by the end of her 12-hour shift.

In the following days and weeks, we were dependent on our friends and family to get us through. People stepped up to do big things for us, like take our dogs into their home indefinitely. People we'd never even met sent us notes of encouragement and gifts for the girls. Yes, we were grateful for the people around us and for the support.

To have a truly grateful heart, in addition to noticing the good things you must also acknowledge them. I once heard an author on a talk show say, "If you really want to tell a man that you love him, say thank you." This stuck with me. Saying thank you for supporting the family, for being a good partner, and for the myriad of things Clay does every day is an excellent way of expressing my love for him. This idea should be expanded to friends and family as well. How often have you thanked your parent for the lessons you've learned? Have you acknowledged a teacher who influenced you? Is there someone who gave you an honest opinion when no one else would? Did someone do something small that made a profound impact on you?

An emailed "thank you" from an American Heart Association staff person in Milwaukee is one of the best examples I could find. As the logistics chair of our local Heart Walk and I spent months working with the staff. Some of the meetings were held at my house while my girls napped. Since it was convenient for me to have everyone come there, I tried to make it a nice experience so they'd agree to do it again. I served snacks and broke out some of the good dishes I'd inherited (they do no good sitting in the cupboard). I had no idea that a simple gesture could mean so much.

From: "Sandy Mazurek"
To: "Eliz Greene"
Subject: You have changed my life
Date: Wed, 8 Dec 2004 11:18:37 -0600

Wow! Does that sound like an eye-catching lead?

It's true in many ways, but this is kind of a small way. Two years ago you invited several staff to your home for a meeting and served tea in an elegant fashion. I have always liked the smell of coffee, but never the taste, and was curious about tea - not curious enough to actually spend $ to buy some but open to the opportunity to try it. Long an addict of Diet Coke I had been thinking I should become more adventuresome. Milk? Yech. Juice? Too sweet. Water? Yeah it's okay but boring.

This little note is to let you know that you have started me on tea. It is now my preferred beverage with sweets.

As I am just enjoying another cup today, I thought I would share that little ripple in the ocean you probably never knew you made.

Thanks

Sandy Mazurek

Her message really touched me and reminded me of how small gestures can make a difference. It is a perfect example of having a grateful heart and moving a little water as well. We all affect the people around us in ways we will never fully know.

Taking the time to acknowledge the things you are grateful for can change the way you see the world.

Reach Out

Sometimes moving the water involves simply reaching out to someone. At first, doctors told me I was the only person ever to survive what had happened to me. There isn't any documentation about cases like mine. Logically, if I hadn't been in the hospital when it happened, I wouldn't have survived. The doctors didn't know of anyone who had. It was a heavy burden. Both Clay and I worried about it happening

again. Leaving the safety of our house was scary and I had to talk myself out of the fear. Clay worried if he didn't know where I was at any given moment. If he called and I didn't pick up the phone, he'd continue to call until I did. This went on for months, until on the day our daughters were baptized, six

months after they were born, I got a call from a woman. She said, "this happened to me too, and you are going to be okay." I'll never be able to thank her for picking up the phone. She reached out to a total stranger and made a difference no one else could. How about that for moving the water?

Paying attention to the people around you and reaching out to them is an essential part of moving the water and living a passionate life. Extending your friendship and comfort is an excellent way to be a positive force in the world. Being open enough to allow others to reach out to you is another. It is often far easier to give help than to receive it. By allowing yourself to be vulnerable, to share your fears and hurts, to allow others to comfort, guide, and help you, you allow such compassion and grace into your life. However, it can leave you feeling a little exposed. Why is it that we equate strength with being stoic and weakness with vulnerability? Yet, the only way to truly connect with other people, and let them know you, is to be open and allow them in. I am honored whenever a friend confides in me, needing my compassion or perspective. I would lose out on so much if I wasn't open in return.

Open your heart, reach out and allow others to reach out to you.

Celebrate

As my fortieth birthday approached, I was amazed at how many people acted as if it was a death sentence. "Oh, FORTY, how awful!" What? Why wouldn't I celebrate another year of life. I mean, really, what is the alternative? Why be unhappy about having spent forty years on this planet? I'm proud of the things I've done and the person I am. Why not celebrate? To let a birthday or anniversary go by unmarked and uncelebrated seems like such a waste to me.

Celebrating life is a big part of being passionate about it. Not only is it a way to acknowledge something wonderful, but it is also a way to share your joy with those around you. Just as it is important to be open enough to share your concerns, sharing your celebrations allows you to connect with others in your life on a deeper level.

About six months after the girls were born, Clay and I celebrated our tenth wedding anniversary. Our lives were crazy with two sixth-month-olds in the house. It would have been so easy to let it go by, but we had so much to be thankful for, so much to celebrate. So even though the house needed to be painted, and the couch was worn out, and I was wearing dresses four sizes larger than I did when we got married, we decided to have a party and do it right. We renewed our vows and had a dinner party for twenty. It meant a lot to both of us to stand before the people who had been so supportive over the last months and pledge our love to each other, again. It meant even more the second time!

Every single person participated in some way during the ceremony and it is something that binds us all together. Clay said he had two regrets from our wedding day: he hadn't given me a really good kiss at the end of the ceremony and he hadn't had the guts to smash the cake into my face. I got a 40s movie star kiss complete with the backwards dip after this ceremony, and later, when he removed his glasses before we cut the cake, I knew I was in trouble. My dress was ruined, but it is an evening I will cherish forever.

However, it's not just the birthdays, anniversaries, graduations, and other big events. It's about celebrating the small moments too. My mom and I play in a golf league in the summer and people always say how much fun it is to play with us. We'll yell and cheer for any kind of decent shot. Really good shots get a big celebration. Golfers know it takes just one decent shot in a round to keep you going. We like to make it fun. It is hard to be grumpy about your game when the people around you are celebrating it.

Clay and I often spend time at the end of the day talking at the kitchen table while the girls play in another room. Oftentimes, we partake in a medicinal glass of red wine - it's good for your heart! Usually there is something we drink a toast to, be it getting the taxes done or his settling a case at work. Sometimes it's to the girls getting through dinner without spilling anything. But it is the little celebrations that make things seem good. It's the high-fives with the girls when they finally figure out how to get their own shoes on. Or going out to dinner, just the two of us, after getting through a particularly busy time. It is taking stock and celebrating what is good. It is paying attention to those around you and helping them celebrate too.

I know I won't get another shot at my fortieth birthday, our next anniversary, or the day the girls figure out how to write their own names. I'm not missing an opportunity to celebrate! Having passion for life is celebrating the big things, the little things, and all the time. What are you celebrating today?

**Celebrate the big things and the little things, too.
Share your joy with the world and let it expand.**

Give Back

Part my passion is giving back for what I've received. I am determined to use my unique perspective and the powerful story I have to tell to make a difference. As a determined and passionate advocate for heart health I give back by:

- Encouraging other women them to take charge of their health
- Advocating for more research dollars to make sure that the new technology is available when the next person needs it.
- Encouraging doctors to trust in their skills and medical judgment, and embrace that new technology for their patients.
- Lobbying for tobacco control and programs to help our children stay away from cigarettes.
- Leading and encouraging others to lead an active, health life.
- Supporting other women who are struggling with heart disease.
- Educating the public about all of these issues.

We all have things we care about. Getting involved in the world around you, and giving back helps bring passion into your life. There is honor and satisfaction in moving the water. How will you move yours? Where does your passion lie?

Discovering ways to give back, even in small ways, allows you to connect with people and make a difference.

Giving back can take all kinds of shapes, from volunteering at your child's school to running for school board. Maybe there is someone at work who needs a mentor. Maybe there is a child who needs a tutor. Sharing your experience, talents and time brings value to them.

Moving the water is a way of connecting with the world around you. While it is important to take care of yourself, it is also important to relate with those around you in a positive way, and allow the positive influence to feed your Passion for Life.

- **Be a Positive Force:** Troll for joy!
- **Have a Grateful Heart.** Notice the good things in your life, be grateful and acknowledge them.
- **Reach Out** to others and allow others into your life.
- **Celebrate.** Share your enjoyment with the world.
- **Give Back.** Connect with the world and make a difference.

However you choose to move the water, leave behind a worthy wake.

Questions to ponder:

Who is the most influential person in your life?

Have you thanked that person?

What do you care about passionately?

How can you share your passion?

What little thing can you celebrate today?

What big thing are you neglecting to celebrate?

Follow In My Wake

**Follow in my wake
You've not that much at stake
For I have plowed the seas
And smoothed the troubled waters**

Yet another song lyric from Jimmy Buffett! This one is from his song "Barometer Soup" and it epitomizes what I hope to accomplish with this book. Mine is not a life to emulate; my path is my own to walk. But I hope the lessons I've learned along the way will help you walk yours.

Early in our friendship, while talking to my friend Kelly about Clay's being out of town, I mentioned being able to make something for dinner I don't get to eat very often because he doesn't like it. She asked what I was making. "Squash," I responded, "but if I really was going to eat what I wanted for dinner, I would just have Oreo's with peanut butter on them!" With a delighted laugh, she exclaimed, "Oh my gosh, you are human!"

With all my talk of exercising every day and eating right and living life with passion, she really thought I had it all together and was so relieved to know I was human, a real person with failings and weaknesses. I admit to a weakness for chocolate and I have no willpower whatsoever to prevent me from eating it if it is in the house. Just like everyone, I have trying days and lose my way. My experience and perspective doesn't make me immune to troubles or grief. I can only use them to help guide me and help me hold on to my perspective and passion.

My wish for you is to take these simple strategies begin to see the happiness and contentment you already have and to seek what you need.

Notice the Wildflowers.

Savor the small moments of happiness you already have in your life. They are there; look and you will find them. Remember to:

- **Breathe.** Slow down enough to see the good things around you.
- **Reflect.** Focus on what is good.
- **Remember.** Hold on to the memory and use it when the wildflowers are hard to find.

Navigate the Path.

Discover what is truly important to you and use it to find your way.

- Use your **Points of Reference** to chart your course.
- **Weigh the Costs** to decide to say "no" to some things in order to emphatically say "yes" to others.

Take Charge.

Be responsible your own happiness. No one will give you what you don't ask for yourself.

- **Take Charge of Your Health** and maintain a body to take you where you want to go.
- **Take Charge of Your Fear** and do the things you want and need to do.
- **Take Charge of Your Needs** and ask for what will make you happy.

Embrace Challenge.

Jump into new things with passion and determination.

- **Embrace a Sense of Humor** and don't let the chance things might not work out stop you.
- **Embrace the Unknown**, have courage to face the adventure.
- **Embrace the Difficult** and focus on the possible.
- **Embrace the Motivation** and get what you deserve.

Move the Water.

Leave your own wake behind.

- **Be a Positive Force**: Troll for Joy.
- **Have a Grateful Heart**. Notice the good things in your life, be grateful and acknowledge them.
- **Reach Out** to others and allow others into your life.
- **Celebrate**. Share your enjoyment with the world.
- **Give Back**. Connect with the world and make a difference.

Above all,
I wish you passion for life.

With Special Thanks...

To Andrew Welyczko, who gets it and used his amazing talents to design this book so others "get it" too. It is beautiful, thank you.

To my Mom, Peggy Hughes, who is always there when we need her and without whom none of this would be possible.

To Juli, Tracy, Kay, Jill and Patty, who asked for my perspective and made me believe I had something valuable to say.

To Juli, Tracy, Tom, Marianne, Joe, Brian, Tricia, Meg, Brad, Sean and Sarah who rushed to our aid and made the worst hours bearable.

To Kelly, I'm running to catch up. Thanks for believing in me.

To Ann Marie Brown, who's support made my recovery possible.

To the doctors, nurses and staff of St. Joseph Regional Medical Center in Milwaukee, Wisconsin, our unending gratitude for your excellent care and personal interest.

To Nancy & Margaret, you saved my life and became my friends.

To everyone who read and commented on *Passion for Life*, especially Lanei, Terri, Colleen, Kay, Tracy, Mike, Kira and Debbie, your time and opinions are greatly appreciated and ever so valuable! Mike, thank you for the honesty. Lanei, if the whole "PhD – college professor-thing" doesn't work out, you have a real future in editing!

To the staff and volunteers of the American Heart Association, your dedication and drive is inspirational.

To the people of Guidant Corporation, thank you for your diligence and innovation. Without Beating Heart, I wouldn't be here.

About The Author

While seven months pregnant with twins, Eliz Greene suffered a massive heart attack - on that day she survived a ten-minute cardiac arrest, the cesarean delivery of her twin daughters, and open-heart surgery.

Known as the "Red Dress Lady", Eliz travels the country delivering inspirational and impassioned speeches on topics relating to heart health and women and heart disease. Eliz's tale of survival and recovery leaves audiences touched and inspired to make simple, yet meaningful, changes in their own lives.

She has lobbied Congress on behalf of the American Heart Association and chairs Wisconsin's AHA State Advocacy Committee. Eliz has been featured in local, national, and international media such as the *Ladies Home Journal*, CNN, and Lifetime.

On the personal side, Eliz balances her speaking career with her other full-time job: raising twin girls! She and her husband, Clay, are avid sailors and triathletes and live in Milwaukee, Wisconsin.

Eliz Greene
Have Red Dress Will Travel
3900 W. Brown Deer Road PMB 185
Milwaukee, WI 53209
414-793-5020
elizgreene@red-dress.net
www.red-dress.net

About The Red Dress

Red is a passionate color.
It symbolizes confidence and change.

The red dress has become the symbol for Women and Heart Disease. Heart disease and stroke are two of the many cardiovascular diseases that kill nearly 500,000 American women each year.

Yet, most women still believe that breast cancer is the biggest threat to their health. The truth is, heart disease and stroke kill more women than the next seven causes of death combined, including all forms of cancer.

Fortunately, there are simple ways to decrease the risk of cardiovascular disease and lead a heart-healthy life.

Red is Eliz's color of choice. As the "Red Dress Lady," she embodies the cause of educating about women and heart disease. Through her speaking business Have Red Dress - Will Travel, and by publishing books and other materials through Red Dress Press, Eliz brings her message to people across the country.

Eliz Greene
Red Dress
3900 W. Brown Deer Road PMB 185
Milwaukee, WI 53209
414-793-5020
elizgreene@red-dress.net
www.red-dress.net

Additional Resources

Please visit the following websites for information and motivation on meeting your goal.

www.americanheart.org
Click links to:

Healthy Lifestyle	Choose To Move
Go Red For Women	You're The Cure (Advocacy)

www.womenheart.org
The national coalition for women with heart disease.

www.nhlbi.nih.gov/health/hearttruth
The National Heart Lung and Blood Institute sponsors The Heart Truth education campaign.

www.shapeup.org
A non-profit organization dedicated to achieving healthy weight for life.

www.thewalkingsite.com
Great tips on walking and fitness

www.4woman.gov
Sponsored by the U.S. Department of Health and Human Services, a great site for women's health issues.

www.wwhf.org
Wisconsin Women's Health Foundation is a great resource.

www.healthyfridge.org
Easy tips for healthy eating.

www.tobaccofreekids.org

www.heartsurgery-usa.com
Information about Beating Heart Surgery and women's heart health issues.

Red Dress Press ~ Order Form

Book **Passion for Life**

Qty: _____ books @ $12.95 ea. $ _____

Booklet **The 100-Day Challenge**

Qty: _____ booklets @ $5.00 ea. $ _____

Sales Tax (5.6% for WI residents only) $ _____

Shipping and Handling $ _____
Within the United States: $2.00 for first item and
$1.00 per each additional item. Please ask about
discounted shipping on large orders.

Total Amount Enclosed $ _____
Check or money order

Shipping information (please print):

Name _____

Address _____

City _____State _____Zip _____

Phone_____

E-Mail _____

Photocopy this form and mail with payment to:

Red Dress Press
3900 W. Brown Deer Road PMB 185
Milwaukee, WI 53209
414.793.5020

Or purchase online at **www.red-dress.net**